THE BEST POEMS OF
JANE KENYON

Also by Jane Kenyon

THE
BEST
POEMS
OF
JANE
KENYON

Selected by Donald Hall

Graywolf Press

Poems included in this volume were previously published in *Collected Poems* by Jane Kenyon (Graywolf Press, 2005).

This selection published by arrangement with the Estate of Donald Hall and the Strothman Agency.

This publication is made possible, in part, by the voters of Minnesota through a Minnesota State Arts Board Operating Support grant, thanks to a legislative appropriation from the arts and cultural heritage fund. Significant support has also been provided by Target, the McKnight Foundation, the Lannan Foundation, the Amazon Literary Partnership, and other generous contributions from foundations, corporations, and individuals. To these organizations and individuals we offer our heartfelt thanks.

Published by Graywolf Press
250 Third Avenue North, Suite 600
Minneapolis, Minnesota 55401

www.graywolfpress.org

Published in the United States of America

ISBN 978-1-64445-019-2

2 4 6 8 9 7 5 3 1
First Graywolf Printing, 2020

Library of Congress Control Number: 2019933487

Cover design: Kyle G. Hunter

Cover photo: Robyn Brown, *Jane Kenyon and Gus* (1989)

Contents

THE BEST POEMS OF
JANE KENYON

From Room to Room

Here in this house, among photographs
of your ancestors, their hymnbooks and old
shoes . . .

       I move from room to room,
a little dazed, like the fly. I watch it
bump against each window.

I am clumsy here, thrusting
slabs of maple into the stove.
Out of my body for a while,
weightless in space. . . .

          Sometimes
the wind against the clapboard
sounds like a car driving up to the house.

My people are not here, my mother
and father, my brother. I talk
to the cats about weather.

"Blessed be the tie that binds . . ."
we sing in the church down the road.
And how does it go from there? The tie . . .

the tether, the hose carrying
oxygen to the astronaut,
turning, turning outside the hatch,
taking a look around.

The Thimble

I found a silver thimble
on the humusy floor of the woodshed,
neither large nor small, the open end
bent oval by the wood's weight,
or because the woman who wore it
shaped it to fit her finger.

Its decorative border of leaves, graceful
and regular, like the edge of acanthus
on the tin ceiling at church . . .
repeating itself over our heads
while we speak in unison
words the wearer must have spoken.

Finding a Long Gray Hair

I scrub the long floorboards
in the kitchen, repeating
the motions of other women
who have lived in this house.
And when I find a long gray hair
floating in the pail,
I feel my life added to theirs.

The Needle

Grandmother, you are as pale
as Christ's hands on the wall above you.
When you close your eyes you are all
white—hair, skin, gown. I blink
to find you again in the bed.

I remember once you told me
you weighed a hundred and twenty-three,
the day you married Grandfather.
You had handsome legs. He watched you
working at the sink.

The soft ring is loose on your hand.
I hated coming here.
I know you can't understand me.
I'll try again,
like the young nurse with the needle.

The Shirt

The shirt touches his neck
and smooths over his back.
It slides down his sides.
It even goes down below his belt—
down into his pants.
Lucky shirt.

From the Back Steps

A bird begins to sing,
hesitates, like a carpenter
pausing to straighten a nail, then
begins again.
The cat lolls in the shade
under the parked car, his head
in the wheel's path.
I bury the thing I love.

But the cat continues to lie
comfortably, right where he is,
and no one will move the car.
My own violence falls away
like paint peeling from a wall.
I am choosing a new color
to paint my house, though I'm still
not sure what the color will be.

Cages

1

Driving to Winter Park in March,
past Cypress Gardens and the baseball camps,
past the dead beagle in the road, his legs
outstretched, as if he meant to walk
on his side in the next life.

At night, the air
smells like a cup of jasmine tea.
The night-bloomer, white
flowering jasmine,
and groves of orange trees
breathing through their sweet skins.

And cattle in the back
of the truck, staggering
as the driver turns off the highway.

2

By the pool, here at the hotel,
animals in cages to amuse us:
monkeys, peacocks, a pair of black swans,
rabbits, parrots, cockatoos,
flamingoes holding themselves on one leg,
perfectly still, as if they loathed
touching the ground.

The black swan floats
in three inches of foul water,
its bright bill thrust under its wing.

And the monkeys: one of them
reaches through the cage
and grabs for my pen, as if
he had finally decided to write a letter
long overdue.

And one lies in the lap of another.
They look like Mary and Jesus
in the Pietà, one searching for fleas
or lice on the other, for succour
on the body of the other—
some particle of comfort, some
consolation for being in this life.

3

And the body, what about the body?
Sometimes it is my favorite child,
uncivilized as those spider monkeys
loose in the trees overhead.

They leap, and cling with their strong
tails, they steal food
from the cages—little bandits.
If Chaucer could see them,

he would change "lecherous as a sparrow"
to "lecherous as a monkey."

And sometimes my body disgusts me.
Filling and emptying it disgusts me.
And when I feel that way
I treat it like a goose with its legs
tied together, stuffing it
until the liver is fat enough
to make a tin of paté.
Then I have to agree that the body
is a cloud before the soul's eye.

This long struggle to be at home
in the body, this difficult friendship.

4

People come here when they are old
for slow walks on the beach
with new companions. Mortuaries
advertise on bus-stop benches.
At night in nearby groves,
unfamiliar constellations
rise in a leafy sky,
and in the parks, mass plantings
of cannas are blooming
their outrageous blooms,
as if speaking final thoughts,
no longer caring what anyone thinks. . . .

At the Feeder

First the Chickadees take
their share, then fly
to the bittersweet vine,
where they crack open the seeds,
excited, like poets
opening the day's mail.

And the Evening Grosbeaks—
those large and prosperous
finches—resemble skiers
with the latest equipment, bright
yellow goggles on their faces.

Now the Bluejay comes in
for a landing, like a SAC bomber
returning to Plattsburgh
after a day of patrolling the ozone.
Every teacup in the pantry rattles.

The solid and graceful bodies
of Nuthatches, perpetually
upside down, like Yogis . . .
and Slate-Colored Juncoes, feeding
on the ground, taking only
what falls to them.

The cats watch, one
from the lid of the breadbox,
another from the piano. A third

flexes its claws in sleep, dreaming
perhaps, of a chicken neck,
or of being worshiped as a god
at Bubastis, during
the XXIII dynasty.

Afternoon in the House

It's quiet here. The cats
sprawl, each
in a favored place.
The geranium leans this way
to see if I'm writing about her:
head all petals, brown
stalks, and those green fans.
So you see,
I am writing about you.

I turn on the radio. Wrong.
Let's not have any noise
in this room, except
the sound of a voice reading a poem.
The cats request
The Meadow Mouse, by Theodore Roethke.

The house settles down on its haunches
for a doze.
I know you are with me, plants,
and cats—and even so, I'm frightened,
sitting in the middle of perfect
possibility.

Full Moon in Winter

Bare branches rise
and fall overhead.
The barn door bangs loose,
persistent as remorse
after anger and shouting.

Dogs bark across the pond.
The shadow of the house
appears on the crusted snow
like the idea of a house,
and my own shadow

lies down in the cold
at my feet, lunatic,
like someone tired
of living in a body,
needy and full of desire. . . .

Year Day

We are living together on the earth.
The clock's heart
beats in its wooden chest.
The cats follow the sun through the house.
We lie down together at night.

Today, you work in your office,
and I in my study. Sometimes
we are busy and casual.
Sitting here, I can see
the path we have made on the rug.

The hermit gives up
after thirty years of hiding in the jungle.
The last door to the last room
comes unlatched. Here are the gestures
of my hands. Wear them in your hair.

The Suitor

We lie back to back. Curtains
lift and fall,
like the chest of someone sleeping.
Wind moves the leaves of the box elder;
they show their light undersides,
turning all at once
like a school of fish.
Suddenly I understand that I am happy.
For months this feeling
has been coming closer, stopping
for short visits, like a timid suitor.

Now That We Live

Fat spider by the door.

Brow of hayfield, blue
eye of pond.
Sky at night like an open well.

Whip-Poor-Will calls
in the tall grass:
I belong to the Queen of Heaven!

The cheerful worm
in the cheerful ground.

Regular shape of meadow and wall
under the blue
                imperturbable mountain.

Indolence in Early Winter

A letter arrives from friends. . . .
Let them all divorce, remarry
and divorce again!
Forgive me if I doze off in my chair.

I should have stoked the stove
an hour ago. The house
will go cold as stone. Wonderful!
I won't have to go on
balancing my checkbook.

Unanswered mail piles up
in drifts, precarious,
and the cat sets everything sliding
when she comes to see me.

I am still here in my chair,
buried under the rubble
of failed marriages, magazine
subscription renewal forms, bills,
lapsed friendships. . . .

This kind of thinking is caused
by the sun. It leaves the sky earlier
every day, and goes off somewhere,
like a troubled husband,
or like a melancholy wife.

Evening at a Country Inn

From here I see a single red cloud
impaled on the Town Hall weather vane.
Now the horses are back in their stalls,
and the dogs are nowhere in sight
that made them run and buck
in the brittle morning light.

You laughed only once all day—
when the cat ate cucumbers
in Chekhov's story . . . and now you smoke
and pace the long hallway downstairs.

The cook is roasting meat for the evening meal,
and the smell rises to all the rooms.
Red-faced skiers stamp past you
on their way in; their hunger is Homeric.

I know you are thinking of the accident—
of picking the slivered glass from his hair.
Just now a truck loaded with hay
stopped at the village store to get gas.
I wish you would look at the hay—
the beautiful sane and solid bales of hay.

Rain in January

I woke before dawn, still
in a body. Water ran
down every window, and rushed
from the eaves.

Beneath the empty feeder
a skunk was prowling for suet
or seed. The lamps flickered off
and then came on again.

Smoke from the chimney
could not rise. It came down
into the yard, and brooded there
on the unlikelihood of reaching

heaven. When my arm slipped
from the arm of the chair
I let it hang beside me, pale,
useless, and strange.

Walking Alone in Late Winter

How long the winter has lasted—like a Mahler
symphony, or an hour in the dentist's chair.
In the fields the grasses are matted
and gray, making me think of June, when hay
and vetch burgeon in the heat, and warm rain
swells the globed buds of the peony.

Ice on the pond breaks into huge planes. One
sticks like a barge gone awry at the neck
of the bridge. . . .The reeds
and shrubby brush along the shore
gleam with ice that shatters when the breeze
moves them. From beyond the bog
the sound of water rushing over trees
felled by the zealous beavers,
who bring them crashing down. . . . Sometimes
it seems they do it just for fun.

Those days of anger and remorse
come back to me; you fidgeting with your ring,
sliding it off, then jabbing it on again.

The wind is keen coming over the ice;
it carries the sound of breaking glass.
And the sun, bright but not warm,
has gone behind the hill. Chill, or the fear
of chill, sends me hurrying home.

The Pond at Dusk

A fly wounds the water but the wound
soon heals. Swallows tilt and twitter
overhead, dropping now and then toward
the outward-radiating evidence of food.

The green haze on the trees changes
into leaves, and what looks like smoke
floating over the neighbor's barn
is only apple blossoms.

But sometimes what looks like disaster
is disaster: the day comes at last,
and the men struggle with the casket
just clearing the pews.

Photograph of a Child on a Vermont Hillside

Beside the rocking horse, for which
she has grown too large,
and the shirts that hang still on the line,
she looks down.
The face is dour and pale
with something private, and will not admit
the journalist, up from Boston
for country color.

How well she knows these hills—
green receding unaccountably to blue—
and the low meadow in middle distance,
buff-colored now, with one
misshapen tree. . . .

What would she say if she cared
to speak a word? a word meaning
childhood is woe in solitude,
and the bliss of turning circles
barefoot in the dusty drive
after the supper dishes are done. . . .

What Came to Me

I took the last
dusty piece of china
out of the barrel.
It was your gravy boat,
with a hard, brown
drop of gravy still
on the porcelain lip.
I grieved for you then
as I never had before.

The Sandy Hole

The infant's coffin no bigger than a flightbag. . . .
The young father steps backward from the sandy hole,
eyes wide and dry, his hand over his mouth.
No one dares to come near him, even to touch his sleeve.

February: Thinking of Flowers

Now wind torments the field,
turning the white surface back
on itself, back and back on itself,
like an animal licking a wound.

Nothing but white—the air, the light;
only one brown milkweed pod
bobbing in the gully, smallest
brown boat on the immense tide.

A single green sprouting thing
would restore me. . . .

Then think of the tall delphinium,
swaying, or the bee when it comes
to the tongue of the burgundy lily.

Mud Season

Here in purgatory bare ground
is visible, except in shady places
where snow prevails.

Still, each day sees
the restoration of another animal:
a sparrow, just now a sleepy wasp;
and, at twilight, the skunk
pokes out of the den,
anxious for mates and meals. . . .

On the floor of the woodshed
the coldest imaginable ooze,
and soon the first shoots
of asparagus will rise,
the fingers of Lazarus. . . .

Earth's open wounds—where the plow
gouged the ground last November—
must be smoothed; some sown
with seed, and all forgotten.

Now the nuthatch spurns the suet,
resuming its diet of flies, and the mesh
bag, limp and greasy, might be taken
down.

Beside the porch step
the crocus prepares an exaltation
of purple, but for the moment
holds its tongue. . . .

Thinking of Madame Bovary

The first hot April day the granite step
was warm. Flies droned in the grass.
When a car went past they rose
in unison, then dropped back down. . . .

I saw that a yellow crocus bud had pierced
a dead oak leaf, then opened wide. How strong
its appetite for the luxury of the sun!

Everyone longs for love's tense joys and red delights.

And then I spied an ant
dragging a ragged, disembodied wing
up the warm brick walk. It must have been
the Methodist in me that leaned forward,
preceded by my shadow, to put a twig just where
the ant was struggling with its own desire.

Camp Evergreen

The boats like huge bright birds
sail back when someone calls them:
the small campers struggle out
and climb the hill to lunch.
I see the last dawdler
disappear in a ridge of trees.

The whole valley sighs
in the haze and heat of noon. Far out
a fish astonishes the air, falls back
into its element. From the marshy cove
the bullfrog offers thoughts
on the proper limits of ambition.

An hour passes. Piano music
comes floating over the water, falters,
begins again, falters. . . .
Only work will make it right.

Some small thing I can't quite see
clatters down through the leafy dome.
Now it is high summer: the solstice:
longed-for, possessed, luxurious, and sad.

The Appointment

The phoebe flew back and forth
between the fencepost and the tree—
not nest-building, just restlessly . . .
and I heard the motorboat on the lake,
going around and through its own wake,
towing the campers two by two.

I thought of a dozen things to do
but rejected them all
in favor of fretting about you.
It might have been the finest day of summer—
the hay was rich and dry, and the breeze
made the heart-shaped leaves of the birch
tell all their secrets,
though they were lost on me. . . .

Bees rummaged through the lilies, methodical
as thieves in a chest of drawers.
I saw them from the chair
nearest the cool foundation stones.
Out of the cellar window came
a draught of damp and evil-smelling air.

The potted geraniums on the porch
hung limp in the blaze of noon. I could
not stir to water them. If you
had turned into the drive just then, even
with cheerful news, I doubt
I could have heard what you had to say.

Alone for a Week

I washed a load of clothes
and hung them out to dry.
Then I went up to town
and busied myself all day.
The sleeve of your best shirt
rose ceremonious
when I drove in; our night-
clothes twined and untwined in
a little gust of wind.

For me it was getting late;
for you, where you were, not.
The harvest moon was full
but sparse clouds made its light
not quite reliable.
The bed on your side seemed
as wide and flat as Kansas;
your pillow plump, cool,
and allegorical. . . .

The Bat

I was reading about rationalism,
the kind of thing we do up north
in early winter, where the sun
leaves work for the day at 4:15.

Maybe the world *is* intelligible
to the rational mind;
and maybe we light the lamps at dusk
for nothing. . . .

Then I heard wings overhead.

The cats and I chased the bat
in circles—living room, kitchen,
pantry, kitchen, living room. . . .
At every turn it evaded us

like the identity of the third person
in the Trinity: the one
who spoke through the prophets,
the one who astounded Mary
by suddenly coming near.

Travel: After a Death

We drove past farms, the hills terraced with sheep.
A rook flapped upward from the stubbled corn:
its shadow fell across my lap one instant
and then was gone. The car was warm. Sleepy,
we passed through Devonshire: sun and showers. . . .
Fields, emerald in January, shone
through leafless hedges, and I watched a man
grasping his plaid cloth cap and walking stick
in one hand, while with perfect courtesy
he sent his dog before him through the stile,
bowing a little like a maître d'.

We found a room in a cold seaside hotel.
The manager had left a sullen girl
—no more than eighteen—and a parakeet
to run his business while he sunned himself
in Portugal. We watched her rip the key
from the wall and fling it toward us. Why,
I wondered, was the front door wedged open
in January, with a raw sea wind
blowing the woolen skirts of the townswomen,
who passed with market baskets on their arms,
their bodies bent forward against the chill
and the steep angle of the cobbled hill?

There were two urns of painted porcelain
flanking the door. A man could stand in one
and still have room for ashes . . . though he'd have
to be a strange man, like the poet Donne,

who pulled a shroud around himself and called
someone to draw—from life—his deathbed scene;
or like Turgenev, who saw bones and skulls
instead of Londoners walking the streets. . . .
Oh, when am I going to own my mind again?

Twilight: After Haying

Yes, long shadows go out
from the bales; and yes, the soul
must part from the body:
what else could it do?

The men sprawl near the baler,
too tired to leave the field.
They talk and smoke,
and the tips of their cigarettes
blaze like small roses
in the night air. (It arrived
and settled among them
before they were aware.)

The moon comes
to count the bales,
and the dispossessed—
Whip-poor-will, Whip-poor-will
—sings from the dusty stubble.

These things happen . . . the soul's bliss
and suffering are bound together
like the grasses. . . .

The last, sweet exhalations
of timothy and vetch
go out with the song of the bird;
the ravaged field
grows wet with dew.

Briefly It Enters, and Briefly Speaks

I am the blossom pressed in a book,
found again after two hundred years. . . .

I am the maker, the lover, and the keeper. . . .

When the young girl who starves
sits down to a table
she will sit beside me. . . .

I am food on the prisoner's plate. . . .

I am water rushing to the wellhead,
filling the pitcher until it spills. . . .

I am the patient gardener
of the dry and weedy garden. . . .

I am the stone step,
the latch, and the working hinge. . . .

I am the heart contracted by joy . . .
the longest hair, white
before the rest. . . .

I am there in the basket of fruit
presented to the widow. . . .

I am the musk rose opening
unattended, the fern on the boggy summit. . . .

I am the one whose love
overcomes you, already with you
when you think to call my name. . . .

Things

The hen flings a single pebble aside
with her yellow, reptilian foot.
Never in eternity the same sound—
a small stone falling on a red leaf.

The juncture of twig and branch,
scarred with lichen, is a gate
we might enter, singing.

The mouse pulls batting
from a hundred-year-old quilt.
She chewed a hole in a blue star
to get it, and now she thrives. . . .
Now is her time to thrive.

Things: simply lasting, then
failing to last: water, a blue heron's
eye, and the light passing
between them: into light all things
must fall, glad at last to have fallen.

Three Songs at the End of Summer

A second crop of hay lies cut
and turned. Five gleaming crows
search and peck between the rows.
They make a low, companionable squawk,
and like midwives and undertakers
possess a weird authority.

Crickets leap from the stubble,
parting before me like the Red Sea.
The garden sprawls and spoils.

Across the lake the campers have learned
to water-ski. They have, or they haven't.
Sounds of the instructor's megaphone
suffuse the hazy air. "Relax! Relax!"

Cloud shadows rush over drying hay,
fences, dusty lane, and railroad ravine.
The first yellowing fronds of goldenrod
brighten the margins of the woods.

Schoolbooks, carpools, pleated skirts;
water, silver-still, and a vee of geese.

⟋

The cicada's dry monotony breaks
over me. The days are bright
and free, bright and free.

Then why did I cry today
for an hour, with my whole
body, the way babies cry?

A white, indifferent morning sky,
and a crow, hectoring from its nest
high in the hemlock, a nest as big
as a laundry basket . . .
                              In my childhood
I stood under a dripping oak,
while autumnal fog eddied around my feet,
waiting for the school bus
with a dread that took my breath away.

The damp dirt road gave off
this same complex organic scent.

I had the new books—words, numbers,
and operations with numbers I did not
comprehend—and crayons, unspoiled
by use, in a blue canvas satchel
with red leather straps.

Spruce, inadequate, and alien
I stood at the side of the road.
It was the only life I had.

In the Grove: The Poet at Ten

She lay on her back in the timothy
and gazed past the doddering
auburn heads of sumac.

A cloud—huge, calm,
and dignified—covered the sun
but did not, could not, put it out.

The light surged back again.

Nothing could rouse her then
from that joy so violent
it was hard to distinguish from pain.

The Pear

There is a moment in middle age
when you grow bored, angered
by your middling mind,
afraid.

That day the sun
burns hot and bright,
making you more desolate.

It happens subtly, as when a pear
spoils from the inside out,
and you may not be aware
until things have gone too far.

Small Early Valentine

Wind plays the spy,
opens and closes doors,
looks behind shutters—
a succession of clatters. I
know perfectly well
where you are: in that
not-here-place you go to,
the antipodes. I have your note
with flights and phone numbers
for the different days. . . .
Dear one, I have made the bed
with the red sheets. Our
dog's the one who lay
on the deep pile of dung,
lifting his head and ears
when after twenty years
Odysseus approached him.

The Blue Bowl

Like primitives we buried the cat
with his bowl. Bare-handed
we scraped sand and gravel
back into the hole.
                                    They fell with a hiss
and thud on his side,
on his long red fur, the white feathers
between his toes, and his
long, not to say aquiline, nose.

We stood and brushed each other off.
There are sorrows keener than these.

Silent the rest of the day, we worked,
ate, stared, and slept. It stormed
all night; now it clears, and a robin
burbles from a dripping bush
like the neighbor who means well
but always says the wrong thing.

We Let the Boat Drift

I set out for the pond, crossing the ravine
where seedling pines start up like sparks
between the disused rails of the Boston and Maine.

The grass in the field would make a second crop
if early autumn rains hadn't washed
the goodness out. After the night's hard frost
it makes a brittle rustling as I walk.

The water is utterly still. Here and there
a black twig sticks up. It's five years today,
and even now I can't accept what cancer did
to him—not death so much as the annihilation
of the whole man, sense by sense, thought
by thought, hope by hope.

Once we talked about the life to come.
I took the Bible from the nightstand
and offered John 14: "I go to prepare
a place for you." "Fine. Good," he said.
"But what about Matthew? 'You, therefore,
must be perfect, as your heavenly Father
is perfect.'" And he wept.

My neighbor honks and waves driving by.
She counsels troubled students; keeps bees;
her goats follow her to the mailbox.

Last Sunday afternoon we went canoeing on the pond.
Something terrible at school had shaken her.
We talked quietly far from shore. The paddles
rested across our laps; glittering drops
fell randomly from their tips. The light
around us seemed alive. A loon—itinerant—
let us get quite close before it dove, coming up
after a long time, and well away from humankind.

April Chores

When I take the chilly tools
from the shed's darkness, I come
out to a world made new
by heat and light.

The snake basks and dozes
on a large flat stone.
It reared and scolded me
for raking too close to its hole.

Like a mad red brain
the involute rhubarb leaf
thinks its way up
through loam.

The Clearing

The dog and I push through the ring
of dripping junipers
to enter the open space high on the hill
where I let him off the leash.

He vaults, snuffling, between tufts of moss;
twigs snap beneath his weight; he rolls
and rubs his jowls on the aromatic earth;
his pink tongue lolls.

I look for sticks of proper heft
to throw for him, while he sits, prim
and earnest in his love, if it is love.

All night a soaking rain, and now the hill
exhales relief, and the fragrance
of warm earth. . . .The sedges
have grown an inch since yesterday,
and ferns unfurled, and even if they try
the lilacs by the barn can't
keep from opening today.

I longed for spring's thousand tender greens,
and the white-throated sparrow's call
that borders on rudeness. Do you know—
since you went away
all I can do
is wait for you to come back to me.

Private Beach

It is always the dispossessed—
someone driving a huge rusted Dodge
that's burning oil, and must cost
twenty-five dollars to fill.

Today before seven I saw, through
the morning fog, his car leave the road,
turning into the field. It must be
his day off, I thought, or he's out
of work and drinking, or getting stoned.
Or maybe as much as anything
he wanted to see
where the lane through the hay goes.

It goes to the bluff overlooking
the lake, where we've cleared
brush, swept the slippery oak
leaves from the path, and tried to destroy
the poison ivy that runs
over the scrubby, sandy knolls.

Sometimes in the evening I'll hear
gunshots or firecrackers. Later a car
needing a new muffler backs out
to the road, headlights withdrawing
from the lowest branches of the pines.

Next day I find beer cans, crushed;
sometimes a few fish too small
to bother cleaning and left
on the moss to die; or the leaking
latex trace of outdoor love. . . .
Once I found the canvas sling chairs
broken up and burned.

Whoever laid the fire gathered stones
to contain it, like a boy pursuing
a merit badge, who has a dream of work,
and proper reward for work.

The Three Susans

Ancient maples mingle over us, leaves
the color of pomegranates.
The days are warm with honey light,
but the last two nights have finished
every garden in the village.

The provident have left green tomatoes
to ripen on newspaper in the darkness of sheds.
The peppers were already in.
Now there will be no more corn.

I let myself through the wrought-iron gate
of the graveyard, and—meaning to exclude
the dog—I close it after me. But he runs
to the other end, and jumps the stone
wall overlooking Elbow Pond.

Here Samuel Smith lay down at last
with his three wives, all named Susan.
I had to see it for myself. They died
in their sixties, one outliving him.
So why do I feel indignant? He suffered.
Love and the Smiths' peculiar fame
"to nothingness do sink." And down the row
Sleepers are living up to their name.

The dog cocks his leg on a stone.
But animals do not mock, and the dead
may be glad to have life breaking in.

The sun drops low over the pond.
Long shadows move out from the stones,
and a chill rises from the moss,
prompt as a deacon. And at Keats's grave
in the Protestant cemetery in Rome
it is already night,
and wild cats are stalking in the moat.

Lines for Akhmatova

The night train from Moscow, beginning to slow,
pulled closer to your sleeping city.
A sound like tiny bells in cold air . . . Then
the attendant appeared with glasses of strong tea.
"Wake up, ladies! This is Leningrad."

The narrow canals gleam black and still
under ornate street lamps, and in the parks
golden leaves lie on the sandy paths
and wooden benches. By light of day
old women dressed in black sweep them away
with birch stick brooms.

Your work, your amorous life, your scholarship—
everything happened here, where the Party
silenced you for twenty-five years
for writing about love—a middle-class activity.

Husband and son, lovers, dear companions
were imprisoned or killed, emigrated or died.
You turned still further inward,
imperturbable as a lion-gate, and lived on
stubbornly, learning Dante by heart.

In the end you outlived the genocidal
Georgian with his mustache thick as a snake.
And in triumph, an old woman, you wrote:
I can't tell if the day is ending, or the world,
or if the secret of secrets is within me again.

September Garden Party

We sit with friends at the round
glass table. The talk is clever;
everyone rises to it. Bees
come to the spiral pear peelings
on your plate.
From my lap or your hand
the spice of our morning's privacy
comes drifting up. Fall sun
passes through the wine.

Father and Son

August. My neighbor started cutting wood
on cool Sabbath afternoons, the blue
plume of the saw's exhaust wavering over
his head. At first I didn't mind the noise
but it came to seem like a species of pain.

From time to time he let the saw idle,
stepping back from the logs and aromatic
dust, while his son kicked the billets
down the sloping drive toward the shed.
In the lull they sometimes talked.

His back ached unrelentingly, he assumed
from all the stooping. Sundays that fall
they bent over the pile of beech and maple,
intent on getting wood for winter, the last,
as it happened, of their life together.

Let Evening Come

Let the light of late afternoon
shine through chinks in the barn, moving
up the bales as the sun moves down.

Let the cricket take up chafing
as a woman takes up her needles
and her yarn. Let evening come.

Let dew collect on the hoe abandoned
in long grass. Let the stars appear
and the moon disclose her silver horn.

Let the fox go back to its sandy den.
Let the wind die down. Let the shed
go black inside. Let evening come.

To the bottle in the ditch, to the scoop
in the oats, to air in the lung
let evening come.

Let it come, as it will, and don't
be afraid. God does not leave us
comfortless, so let evening come.

August Rain, after Haying

Through sere trees and beheaded
grasses the slow rain falls.
Hay fills the barn; only the rake
and one empty wagon are left
in the field. In the ditches
goldenrod bends to the ground.

Even at noon the house is dark.
In my room under the eaves
I hear the steady benevolence
of water washing dust
raised by the haying
from porch and car and garden
chair. We are shorn
and purified, as if tonsured.

The grass resolves to grow again,
receiving the rain to that end,
but my disordered soul thirsts
after something it cannot name.

The Stroller

1949

It was copen blue, strong and bright,
and the metal back looked like caning
on a chair. The peanut-shaped tray
had a bar with sliding beads:
red, yellow, blue, green, white.
It was hard for Mother to push the stroller
on the sandy shoulders of the road.

Sitting in the stroller
in the driveway of the new house
on a morning in early spring, trees
leafing out, I could hear cows
lowing in their stalls across the road,
and see geese hissing and flapping
at a sheep that wandered too close
to the goslings. From the stroller I surveyed
my new domain like a dowager queen.
When something pleased me I kicked
my feet and spun the bright beads.
Spittle dropped from my lower lip
like a spider plunging on its filament.

1991

Mother is moving; we're sorting
through fifty years' accumulations—
a portfolio of Father's drawings
from his brief career in Architecture

School, exercises in light and shadow,
vanishing point; renderings of acanthus
cornices, gargoyles. . . .Then I come upon
a drawing of my stroller, precisely to scale,
just as I remember it.

And here is a self-portrait, looser,
where he wears the T-shirt whose stripes
I know were red and white
although the drawing is pencil.
Beside Father, who sits in a blue chair
that I remember, by a bookcase I remember,
under a lamp I remember, is the empty stroller.

1951

He was forty-seven, a musician
who took other jobs to get by,
a dreamer, a reader, a would-be farmer
with weak lungs from many pneumonias
and from playing cocktail piano
late in smoky bars. On weekend mornings
we crept around so he could sleep until ten.

When he came home from his day-job
at the bookstore, I untied his shoes.
I waited all day to untie them,
wanting no other happiness. I was four.
He never went to town without a suit

and tie, a linen handkerchief
in his pocket, and his shoes
were good leather, the laces themselves
leather. I loved the rich pungency
of his brown, well-shined, warm shoes.

1959

Mother took in sewing.
One by one Ann Arbor's bridge club
ladies found her. They pulled into our drive
in their Thunderbirds and Cadillacs
as I peered down between muslin curtains
from my room. I lay back on the bed, thinking
of nothing in particular, until they went
away. When I came downstairs the scent
of cigarettes and perfume persisted in the air.

One of them I liked. She took
her two dachshunds everywhere
on a bifurcated leash; they hopped comically
up the porch steps and into our house.
She was Italian, from Modena, displaced,
living in Ann Arbor as the wife
of a Chrysler executive. She never wore
anything but beige or gray knits.
She was six feet tall and not ashamed of it,
with long, loose red hair held back
by tortoiseshell combs. She left cigarette

butts in the ashtray with bright red
striated crescents on them.

She was different from the others,
attached to my mother in the way
European women are attached
to their dressmakers and hairdressers.
When she traveled abroad
she brought back classical recordings
and perfume. I thought I would not mind
being like Marcella, though I recognized
that she was lonely. Her husband traveled
frequently, and she had a son
living in Florence who never came "home."
His enterprises were obscure. . . .
Marcella had her dogs, her solitude,
her elegance—at once sedate and slightly
wild—and, it seemed, a new car every time
the old one got dirty, a luxury
to which she seemed oblivious.

1991

Disturbed but full of purpose, we push
Father's indifferent drawings into the trash.
Mother saves the self-portrait and the acanthus
cornice. I save only the rendering
of the stroller, done on tracing paper, diaphanous.

Looking at it
is like looking into a mirror
and seeing your own eyes and someone else's
eyes as well, strange to you
but benign, curious, come
to interrogate your wounds, the progress
of your beating heart.

The Argument

On the way to the village store
I drive through a downdraft
from the neighbor's chimney.
Woodsmoke tumbles from the eaves
backlit by sun, reminding me
of the fire and sulfur of Grandmother's
vengeful God, the one who disapproves
of jeans and shorts for girls,
dancing, strong waters, and adultery.

A moment later the smoke enters
the car, although the windows are tight,
insinuating that I might, like Judas,
and the foolish virgins, and the rich
young man, have been made for unquenchable
fire. God will need something to burn
if the fire is to be unquenchable.

"All things work together for the good
for those who love God," she said
to comfort me at Uncle Hazen's funeral,
where Father held me up to see
the maroon gladiolus that trembled
as we approached the bier, the elaborate
shirred satin, brass fittings, anything,

oh, anything but Uncle's squelched
and made-up face.
"No! NO! How is it good to be dead?"

I cried afterward, wild-eyed and flushed.
"God's ways are not our ways,"
she said then out of pity
and the wish to forestall the argument.

Biscuit

The dog has cleaned his bowl
and his reward is a biscuit,
which I put in his mouth
like a priest offering the host.

I can't bear that trusting face!
He asks for bread, expects
bread, and I in my power
might have given him a stone.

Not Writing

A wasp rises to its papery
nest under the eaves
where it daubs

at the gray shape,
but seems unable
to enter its own house.

Having It Out with Melancholy

> *If many remedies are prescribed for an illness,*
> *you may be certain that the illness has no cure.*
>
> A. P. Chekhov
> *The Cherry Orchard*

1 FROM THE NURSERY

When I was born, you waited
behind a pile of linen in the nursery,
and when we were alone, you lay down
on top of me, pressing
the bile of desolation into every pore.

And from that day on
everything under the sun and moon
made me sad—even the yellow
wooden beads that slid and spun
along a spindle on my crib.

You taught me to exist without gratitude.
You ruined my manners toward God:
"We're here simply to wait for death;
the pleasures of earth are overrated."

I only appeared to belong to my mother,
to live among blocks and cotton undershirts
with snaps; among red tin lunch boxes
and report cards in ugly brown slipcases.
I was already yours—the anti-urge,
the mutilator of souls.

2 BOTTLES

Elavil, Ludiomil, Doxepin,
Norpramin, Prozac, Lithium, Xanax,
Wellbutrin, Parnate, Nardil, Zoloft.
The coated ones smell sweet or have
no smell; the powdery ones smell
like the chemistry lab at school
that made me hold my breath.

3 SUGGESTION FROM A FRIEND

You wouldn't be so depressed
if you really believed in God.

4 OFTEN

Often I go to bed as soon after dinner
as seems adult
(I mean I try to wait for dark)
in order to push away
from the massive pain in sleep's
frail wicker coracle.

5 ONCE THERE WAS LIGHT

Once, in my early thirties, I saw
that I was a speck of light in the great
river of light that undulates through time.

I was floating with the whole
human family. We were all colors—those
who are living now, those who have died,
those who are not yet born. For a few

moments I floated, completely calm,
and I no longer hated having to exist.

Like a crow who smells hot blood
you came flying to pull me out
of the glowing stream.
"I'll hold you up. I never let my dear
ones drown!" After that, I wept for days.

6 IN AND OUT

The dog searches until he finds me
upstairs, lies down with a clatter
of elbows, puts his head on my foot.

Sometimes the sound of his breathing
saves my life—in and out, in
and out; a pause, a long sigh. . . .

7 PARDON

A piece of burned meat
wears my clothes, speaks
in my voice, dispatches obligations
haltingly, or not at all.

It is tired of trying
to be stouthearted, tired
beyond measure.

We move on to the monoamine
oxidase inhibitors. Day and night
I feel as if I had drunk six cups
of coffee, but the pain stops
abruptly. With the wonder
and bitterness of someone pardoned
for a crime she did not commit
I come back to marriage and friends,
to pink-fringed hollyhocks; come back
to my desk, books, and chair.

8 CREDO

Pharmaceutical wonders are at work
but I believe only in this moment
of well-being. Unholy ghost,
you are certain to come again.

Coarse, mean, you'll put your feet
on the coffee table, lean back,
and turn me into someone who can't
take the trouble to speak; someone
who can't sleep, or who does nothing
but sleep; can't read, or call
for an appointment for help.

There is nothing I can do
against your coming.
When I awake, I am still with thee.

9 Wood Thrush

High on Nardil and June light
I wake at four,
waiting greedily for the first
notes of the wood thrush. Easeful air
presses through the screen
with the wild, complex song
of the bird, and I am overcome

by ordinary contentment.
What hurt me so terribly
all my life until this moment?
How I love the small, swiftly
beating heart of the bird
singing in the great maples;
its bright, unequivocal eye.

Chrysanthemums

The doctor averted his eyes
while the diagnosis fell on us,
as though the picture of the girl
hiding from her dog
had suddenly fallen off the wall.
We were speechless all the way home.
The light seemed strange.

A weekend of fear and purging. . . .
Determined to work, he packed his
Dictaphone, a stack of letters,
and a roll of stamps. At last the day
of scalpels, blood, and gauze arrived.

Eyes closed, I lay on his tightly made
bed, waiting. From the hallway I heard
an old man, whose nurse was helping him
to walk: "That Howard Johnson's. It's
nothing but the same thing over and over
again."
          "That's right. It's nothing special."

Late in the afternoon, when slanting
sun betrayed a wad of dust under the bed-
side stand, I heard the sound of casters
and footsteps slowing down.
The attendants asked me to leave the room
while they moved him onto the bed,
and the door remained closed a long time.

Evening came. . . .
While he dozed, fitfully, still stupefied
by anesthetics, I tried to read,
my feet propped on the rails of the bed.
Odette's chrysanthemums
were revealed to me, ranks of them
in the house where Swann, jealousy
constricting his heart, made late-night calls.

And while I read, pausing again
and again to look at him, the smell
of chrysanthemums sent by friends
wavered from the sill, mixing
with the smells of drastic occasions
and disinfected sheets.

He was too out of it
to press the bolus for medication.
Every eight minutes, when he could have
more, I pressed it, and morphine dripped
from the vial in the locked box
into his arm. I made a hive
of eight-minute cells
where he could sleep without pain,
or beyond caring about pain.

Over days the IVs came out,
and freedom came back to him—
walking, shaving, sitting in a chair.
The most ordinary gestures seemed

cause for celebration.
Hazy with analgesics, he read
the *Boston Globe*, and began to talk
on the telephone.

Once the staples were out,
and we had the discharge papers
in hand, I brought him home, numbed up
for the trip. He dozed in the car,
woke, and looked with astonishment
at the hills, gold and quince
under October sun, a sight so
overwhelming that we began to cry,
he first, and then I.

Back

We try a new drug, a new combination
of drugs, and suddenly
I fall into my life again

like a vole picked up by a storm
then dropped three valleys
and two mountains away from home.

I can find my way back. I know
I will recognize the store
where I used to buy milk and gas.

I remember the house and barn,
the rake, the blue cups and plates,
the Russian novels I loved so much,

and the black silk nightgown
that he once thrust
into the toe of my Christmas stocking.

Moving the Frame

Impudent spring has come
since your chest rose and fell
for the last time, bringing
the push and ooze of budding peonies,
with ants crawling over them
exuberantly.

I have framed the picture
from your obituary. It must have been
taken on a hot graduation day:
You're wearing your academic robes
—how splendid they were—
and your hair and beard are curly
with sweat. The tassel sways. . . .
No matter how I move your face
around my desk,
your eyes don't meet my eyes.

There was one hard night
while your breath became shallower
and shallower, and then
you were gone from us. A person
simply vanishes! I came home
and fell deeply asleep for a long
time, but I woke up again.

Not Here

Searching for pillowcases trimmed
with lace that my mother-in-law
once made, I open the chest of drawers
upstairs to find that mice
have chewed the blue and white linen
dishtowels to make their nest,
and bedded themselves
among embroidered dresser scarves
and fingertip towels.

Tufts of fibers, droppings like black
caraway seeds, and the stains of birth
and afterbirth give off the strong
unforgettable attar of mouse
that permeates an old farmhouse
on humid summer days.

A couple of hickory nuts
roll around as I lift out
the linens, while a hail of black
sunflower shells
falls on the pillowcases,
yellow with age, but intact.
I'll bleach them and hang them in the sun
to dry. There's almost no one left
who knows how to crochet lace. . . .

The bright-eyed squatters are not here.
They've scuttled out to the fields

for summer, as they scuttled in
for winter—along the wall, from chair
to skirted chair, making themselves
flat and scarce while the cat
dozed with her paws in the air,
and we read the mail
or evening paper, unaware.

In Memory of Jack

Once, coming down the long hill
into Andover on an autumn night
just before deer season, I stopped
the car abruptly to avoid a doe.

She stood, head down, perhaps twenty
feet away, her legs splayed
as if she meant to stand her ground.

For a long moment she looked
at the car, then bolted right at it,
glancing off the hood with a crash,
into a field of corn stubble.

So I rushed at your illness, your
suffering and death—the bright
lights of annihilation and release.

Insomnia at the Solstice

The quicksilver song
of the wood thrush spills
downhill from ancient maples
at the end of the sun's single most
altruistic day. The woods grow dusky
while the bird's song brightens.

Reading to get sleepy . . . Rabbit
Angstrom knows himself so well,
why isn't he a better man?
I turn out the light, and rejoice
in the sound of high summer, and in air
on bare shoulders—*dolce, dolce*—
no blanket, or even a sheet.
A faint glow remains over the lake.

Now come wordless contemplations
on love and death, worry about
money, and the resolve to have the vet
clean the dog's teeth, though
he'll have to anesthetize him.

An easy rain begins, drips off
the edge of the roof, onto the tin
watering can. A vast irritation rises. . . .
I turn and turn, try one pillow,
two, think of people who have no beds.

A car hisses by on wet macadam.
Then another. The room turns
gray by insensible degrees. The thrush
begins again its outpouring of silver
to rich and poor alike, to the just
and the unjust.

The dog's wet nose appears
on the pillow, pressing lightly,
decorously. He needs to go out.
All right, cleverhead, let's declare
a new day.
              Washing up, I say
to the face in the mirror,
"You're still here! How you bored me
all night, and now I'll have
to entertain you all day. . . ."

Peonies at Dusk

White peonies blooming along the porch
send out light
while the rest of the yard grows dim.

Outrageous flowers as big as human
heads! They're staggered
by their own luxuriance: I had
to prop them up with stakes and twine.

The moist air intensifies their scent,
and the moon moves around the barn
to find out what it's coming from.

In the darkening June evening
I draw a blossom near, and bending close
search it as a woman searches
a loved one's face.

Three Small Oranges

My old flannel nightgown, the elbows out,
one shoulder torn. . . . Instead of putting it
away with the clean wash, I cut it up
for rags, removing the arms and opening
their seams, scissoring across the breast
and upper back, then tearing the thin
cloth of the body into long rectangles.
Suddenly an immense sadness . . .

Making supper, I listen to news
from the war, of torture where the air
is black at noon with burning oil,
and of a market in Baghdad, bombed
by accident, where yesterday an old man
carried in his basket a piece of fish
wrapped in paper and tied with string,
and three small hard green oranges.

Potato

In haste one evening while making dinner
I threw away a potato that was spoiled
on one end. The rest would have been

redeemable. In the yellow garbage pail
it became the consort of coffee grounds,
banana skins, carrot peelings.
I pitched it onto the compost
where steaming scraps and leaves
return, like bodies over time, to earth.

When I flipped the fetid layers with a hay
fork to air the pile, the potato turned up
unfailingly, as if to revile me—

looking plumper, firmer, resurrected
instead of disassembling. It seemed to grow
until I might have made shepherd's pie
for a whole hamlet, people who pass the day
dropping trees, pumping gas, pinning
hand-me-down clothes on the line.

Sleepers in Jaipur

A mango moon climbs the dark
blue sky. In the gutters of a market
a white, untethered cow browses
the day's leavings—wilted greens,
banana peels, spilt rice,
a broken basket.

The sleepers, oh, so many sleepers . . .
They lie on rush mats in their hot
stick hut. The man and woman
want to love wildly, uproariously;
instead, they are quiet and efficient
in the dark. Bangles ring
as his mother stirs in her sleep.

Who can say what will come of
the quickening and slowing
of their breaths on each other's
necks, of their deep shudders?
Another sleeper, a gift of God,
ribs and shoulders to be clothed
in flesh . . .

In the dusty garden the water
she carried from the well in a jug
balanced on her black hair
stares back at the moon
from its cool terra-cotta urn.

Gettysburg: July 1, 1863

The young man, hardly more
than a boy, who fired the shot
had looked at him with an air
not of anger but of concentration,
as if he were surveying a road,
or feeding a length of wood into a saw:
It had to be done just so.

The bullet passed through
his upper chest, below the collarbone.
The pain was not what he might
have feared. Strangely exhilarated
he staggered out of the pasture
and into a grove of trees.

He pressed and pressed
the wound, trying to stanch
the blood, but he could only press
what he could reach, and he could
not reach his back, where the bullet
had exited.
        He lay on the earth
smelling the leaves and mosses,
musty and damp and cool
after the blaze of open afternoon.

How good the earth smelled,
as it had when he was a boy
hiding from his father,

who was intent on strapping him
for doing his chores
late one time too many.

A cowbird razzed from a rail fence.
It isn't mockery, he thought,
no malice in it . . . just a noise.
Stray bullets nicked the oaks
overhead. Leaves and splinters fell.

Someone near him groaned.
But it was his own voice he heard.
His fingers and feet tingled,
the roof of his mouth,
and the bridge of his nose. . . .

He became dry, dry, and thought
of Christ, who said, *I thirst.*
His man-smell, the smell of his hair
and skin, his sweat, the salt smell
of his cock and the little ferny hairs
that two women had known

left him, and a sharp, almost sweet
smell began to rise from his open mouth
in the warm shade of the oaks.
A streak of sun climbed the rough
trunk of a tree, but he did not
see it with his open eye.

Pharaoh

"The future ain't what it used to be,"
said the sage of the New York Yankees
as he pounded his mitt, releasing
the red dust of the infield
into the harshly illuminated evening air.

Big hands. Men with big hands
make things happen. The surgeon,
when I asked how big your tumor was,
held forth his substantial fist
with its globed class ring.

Home again, we live as charily as strangers.
Things are off: Touch rankles, food
is not good. Even the kindness of friends
turns burdensome; their flowers sadden
us, so many and so fair.

I woke in the night to see your
diminished bulk lying beside me—
you on your back, like a sarcophagus
as your feet held up the covers. . . .
The things you might need in the next
life surrounded you—your comb and glasses,
water, a book and a pen.

Otherwise

I got out of bed
on two strong legs.
It might have been
otherwise. I ate
cereal, sweet
milk, ripe, flawless
peach. It might
have been otherwise.
I took the dog uphill
to the birch wood.
All morning I did
the work I love.

At noon I lay down
with my mate. It might
have been otherwise.
We ate dinner together
at a table with silver
candlesticks. It might
have been otherwise.
I slept in a bed
in a room with paintings
on the walls, and
planned another day
just like this day.
But one day, I know,
it will be otherwise.

Notes from the Other Side

I divested myself of despair
and fear when I came here.

Now there is no more catching
one's own eye in the mirror,

there are no bad books, no plastic,
no insurance premiums, and of course

no illness. Contrition
does not exist, nor gnashing

of teeth. No one howls as the first
clod of earth hits the casket.

The poor we no longer have with us.
Our calm hearts strike only the hour,

and God, as promised, proves
to be mercy clothed in light.

Happiness

There's just no accounting for happiness,
or the way it turns up like a prodigal
who comes back to the dust at your feet
having squandered a fortune far away.

And how can you not forgive?
You make a feast in honor of what
was lost, and take from its place the finest
garment, which you saved for an occasion
you could not imagine, and you weep night and day
to know that you were not abandoned,
that happiness saved its most extreme form
for you alone.

No, happiness is the uncle you never
knew about, who flies a single-engine plane
onto the grassy landing strip, hitchhikes
into town, and inquires at every door
until he finds you asleep midafternoon
as you so often are during the unmerciful
hours of your despair.

It comes to the monk in his cell.
It comes to the woman sweeping the street
with a birch broom, to the child
whose mother has passed out from drink.
It comes to the lover, to the dog chewing
a sock, to the pusher, to the basket maker,

and to the clerk stacking cans of carrots
in the night.
           It even comes to the boulder
in the perpetual shade of pine barrens,
to rain falling on the open sea,
to the wineglass, weary of holding wine.

In the Nursing Home

She is like a horse grazing
a hill pasture that someone makes
smaller by coming every night
to pull the fences in and in.

She has stopped running wide loops,
stopped even the tight circles.
She drops her head to feed; grass
is dust, and the creekbed's dry.

Master, come with your light
halter. Come and bring her in.

Prognosis

I walked alone in the chill of dawn
while my mind leapt, as the teachers

of detachment say, like a drunken
monkey. Then a gray shape, an owl,

passed overhead. An owl is not
like a crow. A crow makes convivial

chuckings as it flies,
but the owl flew well beyond me

before I heard it coming, and when it
settled, the bough did not sway.

Afternoon at MacDowell

On a windy summer day the well-dressed
trustees occupy the first row
under the yellow and white striped canopy.
Their drive for capital is over,
and for a while this refuge is secure.

Thin after your second surgery, you wear
the gray summer suit we bought eight
years ago for momentous occasions
in warm weather. My hands rest in my lap,
under the fine cotton shawl embroidered
with mirrors that we bargained for last fall
in Bombay, unaware of your sickness.

The legs of our chairs poke holes
in the lawn. The sun goes in and out
of the grand clouds, making the air alive
with golden light, and then, as if heaven's
spirits had fallen, everything's somber again.

After music and poetry we walk to the car.
I believe in the miracles of art, but what
prodigy will keep you safe beside me,
fumbling with the radio while you drive
to find late innings of a Red Sox game?

Dutch Interiors

for Caroline

Christ has been done to death
in the cold reaches of northern Europe
a thousand thousand times.
                                    Suddenly bread
and cheese appear on a plate
beside a gleaming pewter beaker of beer.

Now tell me that the Holy Ghost
does not reside in the play of light
on cutlery!

A woman makes lace,
with a moist-eyed spaniel lying
at her small shapely feet.
Even the maid with the chamber pot
is here; the naughty, red-cheeked girl. . . .

And the merchant's wife, still
in her yellow dressing gown
at noon, dips her quill into India ink
with an air of cautious pleasure.

Reading Aloud to My Father

I chose the book haphazard
from the shelf, but with Nabokov's first
sentence I knew it wasn't the thing
to read to a dying man:
The cradle rocks above an abyss, it began,
*and common sense tells us that our existence
is but a brief crack of light
between two eternities of darkness.*

The words disturbed both of us immediately,
and I stopped. With music it was the same—
Chopin's Piano Concerto—he asked me
to turn it off. He ceased eating, and drank
little, while the tumors briskly appropriated
what was left of him.

But to return to the cradle rocking. I think
Nabokov had it wrong. This is the abyss.
That's why babies howl at birth,
and why the dying so often reach
for something only they can apprehend.

At the end they don't want their hands
to be under the covers, and if you should put
your hand on theirs in a tentative gesture
of solidarity, they'll pull the hand free;
and you must honor that desire,
and let them pull it free.

Woman, Why Are You Weeping?

The morning after the crucifixion,
Mary Magdalene came to see the body
of Christ. She found the stone
rolled away from an empty tomb. Two
figures dressed in white asked her,
"Woman, why are you weeping?"

"Because," she replied, "they have
taken away my Lord, and I don't know
where they have laid him."

Returned from long travel, I sit
in the familiar, sun-streaked pew, waiting
for the bread and wine of Holy Communion.
The old comfort does not rise in me, only
apathy and bafflement.
                        India, with her ceaseless
bells and fire; her crows calling stridently
all night; India with her sandalwood
smoke, and graceful gods, many-headed and many-
armed, has taken away the one who blessed
and kept me.
                The thing is done, as surely
as if my luggage had been stolen from the train.
Men and women with faces as calm as lakes at dusk
have taken away my Lord, and I don't know
where to find him.

What is Brahman? I don't know Brahman.
I don't know *saccidandana*, the bliss
of the absolute and unknowable.
I only know that I have lost the Lord
in whose image I was made.

Whom shall I thank for this pear,
sweet and white? Food *is* God, *Prasadam*,
God's mercy. But who is this God?
The one who is *not this, not that*?

The absurdity of all religious forms
breaks over me, as the absurdity of language
made me feel faint the day I heard friends
giving commands to their neighbor's dog
in Spanish. . . . At first I laughed,
but then I became frightened.

They have taken away my Lord, a person
whose life I held inside me. I saw him
heal, and teach, and eat among sinners.
I saw him break the sabbath to make a higher
sabbath. I saw him lose his temper.

I knew his anguish when he called, "I thirst!"
and received vinegar to drink. The Bible
does not say it, but I am sure he turned

his head away. Not long after he cried, "My God,
my God, why have you forsaken me?"

I watched him reveal himself risen
to Magdalene with a single word: "Mary!"

It was my habit to speak to him. His goodness
perfumed my life. I loved the Lord, he heard
my cry, and he loved me as his own.

    ➤

A man sleeps on the pavement, on a raffia mat—
the only thing that has not been stolen from him.
This stranger who loves what cannot be understood
has put out my light with his calm face.

Shall the fire answer my fears and vapors?
The fire cares nothing for my illness,
nor does Brahma, the creator, nor Shiva who sees
evil with his terrible third eye; Vishnu,
the protector, does not protect me.

I've brought home the smell of the streets
in the folds of soft, bright cotton garments.
When I iron them the steam brings back
the complex odors that rise from the gutters,
of tuberoses, urine, dust, joss, and death.

    ➤

On a curb in Allahabad the family gathers
under a dusty tree, a few quilts hung
between lightposts and a wattle fence
for privacy. Eleven sit or lie around the fire
while a woman of sixty stirs a huge pot.
Rice cooks in a narrow-necked crock
on the embers. A small dog, with patches of bald,
red skin on his back, lies on the corner
of the piece of canvas that serves as flooring.

Looking at them I lose my place.
I don't know why I was born, or why
I live in a house in New England, or why I am
a visitor with heavy luggage giving lectures
for the State Department. Why am I not
tap-tapping with my fingernail
on the rolled-up window of a white Government car,
a baby in my arms, drugged to look feverish?

Rajiv did not weep. He did not cover
his face with his hands when we rowed past
the dead body of a newborn nudging the grassy
banks at Benares—close by a snake
rearing up, and a cast-off garland of flowers.

He explained. When a family are too poor
to cremate their dead, they bring the body

here, and slip it into the waters of the Ganges
and Yamuna rivers.
                    Perhaps the child was dead
at birth; perhaps it had the misfortune
to be born a girl. The mother may have walked
two days with her baby's body to this place
where Gandhi's ashes once struck the waves
with a sound like gravel being scuffed
over the edge of a bridge.

"What shall we do about this?" I asked
my God, who even then was leaving me. The reply
was scorching wind, lapping of water, pull
of the black oarsmen on the oars. . . .

The Sick Wife

The sick wife stayed in the car
while he bought a few groceries.
Not yet fifty,
she had learned what it's like
not to be able to button a button.

It was the middle of the day—
and so only mothers with small children
or retired couples
stepped through the muddy parking lot.

Dry cleaning swung and gleamed on hangers
in the cars of the prosperous.
How easily they moved—
with such freedom,
even the old and relatively infirm.

The windows began to steam up.
The cars on either side of her
pulled away so briskly
that it made her sick at heart.

JANE KENYON (1947–1995) was born in Ann Arbor and gradu-
ated from the University of Michigan. She published four col-
lections of poetry during her lifetime—*From Room to Room*, *The
Boat of Quiet Hours*, *Let Evening Come*, and *Constance*—and a
volume of translations, *Twenty Poems of Anna Akhmatova*. She was
awarded a Guggenheim Fellowship and the PEN Voelcker Award,
and was featured with her husband, Donald Hall, in the Emmy
Award–winning Bill Moyers special "A Life Together." Since her
death, Kenyon's poetry has been published in two celebrated
books, *Otherwise: New & Selected Poems* and *Collected Poems*. *A
Hundred White Daffodils* collects her essays, interviews, newspaper
columns, and other work. She lived in Wilmot, New Hampshire,
until her death in 1995.

The text of *The Best Poems of Jane Kenyon* is set in Adobe Garamond Pro. Book design by Rachel Holscher. Composition by Bookmobile Design and Digital Publisher Services, Minneapolis, Minnesota. Manufactured by Sheridan on acid-free, 30 percent postconsumer wastepaper.